EPIC JOURNEYS

Incredible Tales of Amazing Trails

Written by Sam G. C.
Illustrated by Raquel Martín

Translation from Spanish by Juan Diego Otero

Typefaces: Bazar by Olinda Martins and Rubik by Philipp Hubert and Sebastian Fischer at Hubert & Fischer

Printed by Agpograf, Barcelona, Spain
Made in Europe

Published by Little Gestalten, Berlin, 2024
ISBN 978-3-96704-766-0

For more information, and to order books, please visit gestalten.com/collections/little-gestalten

Bibliographic information published by the Deutsche Nationalbibliothek.

The Deutsche Nationalbibliothek lists this publication in the Deutsche Nationalbibliografie; detailed bibliographic data are available online at dnb.de.

This book was printed on paper certified according to the standards of the FSC®.

MIX
Paper from responsible sources
FSC
www.fsc.org
FSC® C104592

Sam G.C. • Raquel Martín

EPIC JOURNEYS

Incredible Tales of Amazing Trails

INTRODUCTION

We humans are part of a restless species. You can tell that by taking a look at the past few thousand years.

Traveling has always been synonymous with dreaming.

The need to explore beyond new frontiers has taken us a long way, from climbing impossible peaks to traversing the seas.

Our planet was once a blank map, until one fine day, some brave souls left their homes in search of "something more," the wide blue yonder, blazing the trail for everyone else.

While the first nomads set off in search of food, other groups traveled for different reasons: trade, mass migrations, pleasure, or simply to explore and discover new territories.

Traveling makes us feel free, it unites us as a species, opening our minds to the unknown and teaching us to respect both the landscape that surrounds us and the people who inhabit it.

We have traced many routes throughout the millennia, along lines that may not seem like much when you draw them on a map: Is it a path? A starting point and a destination?

With this book, we want to show you a small sample of the diverse and colorful network of routes that have existed for millennia. Journeys that have been recorded in books and have inspired novels, songs, and much more…

Yes, we're sure it will make you a little jealous and eager to get your suitcases out of the closet, don your explorer's vest, and hit the road. But if you can't do that for some reason, we invite you to close your eyes and imagine those places while you run your finger along the lines on the map. And of course, you're allowed to stray from the path.

R. and S.

"Travel enables us to enrich our lives with new experiences, to enjoy and to be educated, to learn respect for foreign cultures, to establish friendships, and above all to contribute to international cooperation and peace throughout the world."

Jules Verne

14 THE ICEFIELDS PARKWAY

22 THE OREGON TRAIL

THE CATHAR TRAIL

26

32 ROUTE 66

16 THE CAMINO DE SANTIAGO

30

THE MAYA ROUTE

40

THE INCA TRAIL

34

THE SPICE ROUTES (BY SEA)

ENJOY THE TRIP!

38 THE TRANS-SIBERIAN RAILWAY

20 THE APPIAN WAY

THE SILK ROAD **10**

28 THE SHIKOKU PILGRIMAGE (SHIKOKU HENRO)

42 THE NILE RIVER ROUTE

THE TEA HORSE ROAD **18**

44 THE GARDEN ROUTE

THE SILK ROAD

In around the first century BCE, the Silk Road was formed as a network of trade routes connecting the East with the West. It served as a bridge over which was carried not only the silk for which it is known, but also tea, iron, porcelain, and even more valuable goods: culture, philosophy, and innovations.

Traveling along with the merchants were religious people, artists, and outlaws. The route also facilitated massive migratory movements that brought tools, products, and new farming methods that were previously unknown in the West, which in turn enabled a process of cultural and technological globalization whose effects can still be felt today.

The term Silk Road *(Seidenstrasse)* was coined by the German geographer Ferdinand von Richthofen in the nineteenth century.

THE LONG ROAD

Traveling along the Silk Road could take anywhere from several months to a year, depending on the stretch you covered and the detours you took. It started from Chang'an (now Xi'an), in China, headed northwest, passing through the Hexi Corridor to the south of the Gobi Desert, until it reached the city of Dunhuang. There, it split into two roads bordering the Taklamakan Desert to the north and south.

The Northern Silk Road ran across the desert until Hami, while the Southern Silk Road followed the northern wall of Tibet along the edge of the desert. Some of the inventions that reached the West via the Silk Road were paper and its production techniques, printing techniques, gunpowder, and the compass.

THE SECRETS OF SILK

In ancient China, the process of silk production was a closely guarded secret and revealing it was punishable by death. Such was the story of a Chinese princess in the third century who, it is said, sold the secret to Japan and was condemned for high treason.

- ×**TYPE OF ROUTE** Commercial
- ×**MODE OF TRANSPORTATION** Horse or camel-drawn caravans
- ×**YEARS** 100 BCE to 1453
- ×**DISTANCE** 4,000 mi (6,400 km)
- ×**STARTING POINT** Chang'an (today's Xi'an)
- ×**END POINT** Constantinople (today's Istanbul)
- ×**EST. TIME TO COMPLETE** Several months to a year

MARCO POLO (1254–1324)

Marco Polo was undoubtedly the most famous explorer and trader to frequent the Silk Road. He traveled and traded throughout the East with his father and uncle for 17 years. When he returned to his hometown of Venice, a war had broken out against Genoa and he was captured and imprisoned for three years. During that time, he recounted his adventures to his close friend and cellmate Rustichello da Pisa, who transcribed them in *The Travels of Marco Polo*.

CARAVANS ON THE SILK ROAD

One of the most common ways of traveling on the road was by camel (although elephants and horses were used as well). The travelers rode on Bactrian camels (two-humped, domesticated camels that were used as pack animals) arranged five to twelve in a column, with each of their heads attached to the tail of the camel in front of them with rope. This train of animals was called a caravan and helped to prevent anyone from stealing the camels and the valuable merchandise they were carrying.

Camels are very strong and can carry up to 600 pounds (270 kilograms) on their backs. Balancing and securing the entire load so that it doesn't fall off during the journey is quite an art form!

Today Bactrian camels are still commonly used as pack animals and can be found mostly in Asia.

THE POWER OF SILK

Silk thread is particularly strong and elastic. It can be stretched to up to 20 times its natural length.

Silkworm cocoons are about an inch (2.5 centimeters) long and made of thread measuring up to 4,000 feet (1,200 meters)!

TAKLAMAKAN

This is the second-largest desert in the world (after the Sahara) and one of the most inhospitable places on the planet. It has some of the most extreme weather conditions seen anywhere.

ALONG THE SILK ROAD
PLACES TO DREAM

Samarkand is one of the oldest continuously inhabited cities in the world. Known for its beauty and ornate architecture, it was the capital of the Islamic Persian empire led by the fearsome conqueror Tamerlane and also the site of his mausoleum, the Gur-e Amir. It was built by the best craftsmen brought in from all over the empire and prospered thanks to the millions of merchants and pilgrims who visited the city on their way along the Silk Road.

SAMARKAND, UZBEKISTAN

Kashgar is the westernmost city in China and was one of the most important trading centers along the Silk Road. It's located between the desert and famous for its huge weekly market (still held on Sundays): according to a local saying, it's a place where you can "buy everything but chicken milk and cow's eggs."

DUNHUANG
THE CRESCENT LAKE

Located 4 miles (about 6.5 kilometers) from the city of Dunhuang, on the edge of the Taklamakan Desert, this dreamy oasis was the perfect place for traders and travelers to take a rest and replenish their supplies.

The Buddhist temple that stands nestled in the crescent today is a reconstruction, as the original one was torn down during the Cultural Revolution of 1966–76 in China.

The lake lies among the Singing Sand Dunes, which seem to defy gravity—some of them rise to be more than 5,000 feet (1,700 meters) high. Their name alludes to the whistling or humming sound that can be heard when the sand grains shuffle down the slopes of the dunes.

SUNWAPTA FALLS

The upper falls, which are easily accessible from the parking lot at the lookout, have an impressive drop of about 60 feet (18 meters). A short hike through a forest of gnarled pine trees comes to an end at the lower falls. From there you can see three waterfalls spread out over the Sunwapta River.

ATHABASCA GLACIER

Standing at the foot of the Athabasca Glacier is amazing. The spectacular scenery, the imposing peaks, the massive ice caves … you feel so small standing in front of this enormous glacier. You can even hear the ice moving and cracking.

THE BOREAL CARIBOU

Also known as the "gray ghost," this caribou, native to Canada, is on the verge of extinction. They are elusive creatures that seek out places uninhabited by humans. In 2019, the Canadian government signed a landmark agreement to protect them.

THE ICEFIELDS PARKWAY

Rated one of the best drives in the world, the Icefields Parkway in Canada is a 144-mile (232-kilometer) stretch of two-lane road that meanders between the towering peaks of the Rocky Mountains, past ice fields, and through the vast valleys between the Banff and Jasper national parks.

This short route is home to more than 100 places of interest, including ancient glaciers, waterfalls, spectacular rock formations, and emerald lakes nested in valleys with dense forests of pine and larch trees.

BOW LAKE

Bow Lake sits at an elevation of 6,300 feet (1,920 meters) and remains frozen for most of the year, which makes it a popular spot for winter activities such as snowshoeing and cross-country skiing.

- ×**TYPE OF ROUTE** Tourist
- ×**MODE OF TRANSPORTATION** Car
- ×**YEAR** Since 1940
- ×**DISTANCE** 144 mi (232 km)
- ×**STARTING POINT** Lake Louise
- ×**END POINT** Jasper
- ×**EST. TIME TO COMPLETE** 3 or 4 days (recommended)

THE CATHEDRAL

OF SANTIAGO DE COMPOSTELA

This huge cathedral, dating back to 1075 and now with an area of 247,570 square feet (23,000 square meters), was designed by Master Mateo. It has three naves and is set within the squares of Obradoiro, Platerías, and Quintana. Inside lie the tombs of St. James and his two disciples, Theodore and Athanasius. Such a building has a tremendous impact on pilgrims arriving there after an exhausting journey. It's impossible not to get a little emotional!

THE COMPOSTELA

The Compostela is an official accreditation issued by the cathedral chapter to people who have completed the pilgrimage. The presentation of this accreditation is one of the most special moments for those who arrive in Santiago.

To certify their passage along any stretch of the Camino, pilgrims have to collect stamps on a Credencial del Peregrino (Pilgrim's Accreditation), a document that needs to be stamped twice a day by the hostels, parishes, associations of friends of the Camino, or post offices along the route. To obtain the Compostela, pilgrims have to cover at least 60 miles (100 kilometers) on foot or 120 miles (200 kilometers) by bicycle.

HOSTELS

After walking along trails and roads all day, the sight of a nearby hostel brings relief to weary travelers. They provide a place for pilgrims to rest and meet, where they not only eat and sleep, but also share their dreams and stories.

Thanks to the rise in popularity of the Camino since 1990, hostels have been popping up all along the routes, meaning it's much easier for pilgrims to find a bed for the night now.

CAMINO DE SANTIAGO

JAMES THE GREATER

In about 813–20, a hermit swore he had seen lights shining on an uninhabited mountain. It was in Compostela, where the tomb of St. James (also known as James the Greater) and his disciples were then found. King Alfonso II of Asturias ordered the construction of a church on top of the tomb. Pilgrims adopted the scallop shells and the staff associated with the apostle as symbols of the pilgrimage.

THE CAMINO DE SANTIAGO

People say that the Camino starts from your own home—they say this because the original route would have been taken by pilgrims starting from many different places! In fact, it comprises an extensive network of routes and itineraries scattered throughout Europe. Currently, there are 281 cataloged Caminos with more than 51,000 miles (83,000 kilometers) of routes. Every year, more than 300,000 pilgrims traipse along the stone paths and country trails and through the forests and vineyards that lead to the Cathedral of Santiago de Compostela in northwestern Spain.

MANY PATHS, BUT ONLY ONE DESTINATION

There are other routes besides the well-known French Way, and throughout history pilgrims have come from all over Europe, traveling on horseback, on foot, or even by sea. There's the Portuguese Way, which starts from Lisbon and is about 386 miles (620 kilometers) long; the Coastal Portuguese Way, about 174 miles (280 kilometers) long; the Northern Way, used in the Middle Ages—and the longest of all at 509 miles (820 kilometers); the Primitivo Way, which starts from Oviedo and was the original way; and the English Way, where pilgrims used to arrive by boat at Ferrol or A Coruña in Spain and which is about 75 miles (120 kilometers) long.

Whichever route you choose, you will always find helpful signage—yellow arrows, shells or signs blue and yellow all point to a single destination.

×**TYPE OF ROUTE** Pilgrimage
×**MODE OF TRANSPORTATION** On foot or by bicycle
×**YEAR** Since the 9th century
×**DISTANCE (FRENCH WAY)** Around 500 mi (800 km)
×**STARTING POINT (FRENCH WAY)** Roncesvalles
×**END POINT** Santiago de Compostela Cathedral
×**EST. TIME TO COMPLETE** 1 month on foot, 10 to 14 days by bicycle

THE TEA HORSE ROAD

× TYPE OF ROUTE Commercial
× MODE OF TRANSPORTATION Mule, horse, or on foot
× YEAR 6th to 20th century
× DISTANCE 1,400 mi (2,300 km)
× STARTING POINT Yunnan, China
× END POINT Tibet

The Tea Horse Road was a network of roads through Tibet, China, and India. Most traders set off with their mules loaded up with sacks of tea from Pu-erh, in southern Yunnan province, where the tea was grown, and then returned from Tibet with horses.

The journey was perilous, spanning about 1,400 miles (2,300 kilometers) across rugged mountains, cliffs, and rivers. Just as on the Silk Road, there were key points along the way for restocking and exchanging goods.

TEA BRICKS

The famous Pu-erh tea became a staple of the Chinese diet as early as the Tang Dynasty (618–907). Black tea, which retains its flavor for a long time, came to be used as a form of currency. It was pressed into bricks and stamped with an imperial seal that marked its quality and price.

POTALA PALACE, LHASA

Lhasa was the nerve center of the route. Merchants from China, Tibet, and India met there to exchange tea, horses, salt, and medicinal goods. The capital of Tibet, Lhasa grew and grew until, in the seventh century, the Potala Palace was built, an icon of Tibetan Buddhism and the residence of the Dalai Lamas until 1959. In 1994, it was named a Unesco World Heritage site.

MENGDING MOUNTAIN

This is the birthplace of tea culture. Legend has it that it is where the Taoist master Wu Lizhen was the first to grow tea and use it for medicinal purposes. Tea from Mengding Mountain is considered sacred. Today, it is home to a tea history museum that showcases tea-related poems, books, and utensils—as well as samples of the region's tea, of course.

THE APPIAN WAY

Also called *Regina Viarum* (the queen of roads), the Appian Way was the first road built by the Romans to connect the Italian capital with Capua, in the south of the country. Over the years it was extended to reach Brindisi, a strategic military position and well known commercial port in the "heel" of Italy. The road was named after the statesman Appius Claudius, who ordered the construction of its first 56 miles (90 kilometers).

The road seems to be frozen in time, inviting you to visit the countless historical sites, tombs, mausoleums, and ancient villas to be found along its route.

THE TOMB OF THE SCIPIOS

The Scipios were one of Rome's most influential dynasties and shaped the course of the empire both militarily and politically. Their tomb was built in the third century BCE and contains 30 sarcophagi as well as the statues of Scipio Africanus (who defeated Hannibal), the poet Quintus Ennius, and Scipio Asiaticus.

THE ARCHAEOLOGICAL PARK OF APPIA ANTICA

This site is like an open-air museum where curious visitors can discover a wealth of historical treasures, ruins, and monuments. It is also the location of the Tombs of Via Latina and the Villa of the Quintilii. This was the largest residential area in the suburbs of Rome and was confiscated by the empire after the Quintilian brothers conspired against Emperor Commodus. Its gardens, architecture, and sculptural decorations are still beautifully preserved.

THE CATACOMBS OF SAN SEBASTIANO

The Catacombs of San Sebastiano span over 7 miles (12 kilometers) of passages and tunnels that can still be visited to this day. Along their walls you can see frescoes, other paintings, and even a bust of the saint. Originally this cemetery was named ad Catacumbas (meaning near the ravine) because of the nearby quarries, making it the first underground burial ground to be called catacombs.

×TYPE OF ROUTE Commercial
×MODE OF TRANSPORTATION On foot or by bicycle
×YEAR Since 312 BCE
×DISTANCE 335 mi (540 km)
×STARTING POINT Rome
×END POINT Brindisi
×EST. TIME TO COMPLETE 30 days on foot; 18 days by bicycle

THE OREGON TRAIL

This was the main route used by settlers during the Great Migration to the American West (1840–60). From its starting point in the city of Independence, Missouri, and stretching over more than 1,800 miles (3,000 kilometers), the trail crossed mountains, rivers, and extremely arid areas. Its destination was the promised land of Oregon.

THE LEWIS AND CLARK EXPEDITION

In 1803, the US president, Thomas Jefferson, sent Captain Meriwether Lewis and Lieutenant William Clark on the challenging mission of exploring the unknown territory of Oregon and the Pacific Northwest. Calling themselves the Corps of Discovery, Lewis and Clark (and the 50 other members of the Corps) took two years to get to the Pacific Ocean and back.

Without the help of Sacagawea, a Native American woman of the Shoshone tribe, they would never have made it. She introduced Lewis and Clark to her people, served as their interpreter, and procured horses for them. On their journey, they met other tribes, handed out gifts, and promised to continue trading in peace.

THE GREAT MIGRATION

The Great Migration from east to west began in about 1843. That year 1,000 people, traveling in a caravan of more than 100 wagons, set off in search of a new home, taking ample provisions with them. Both the US government and the fur traders assured them that they would find more fertile and abundant land in the west. Over the next 40 years thousands of farming and merchant families made the journey.

OREGON: THE PROMISED LAND

When the first settlers arrived in Oregon, they were able to claim the land without paying a cent, with married couples entitled to larger parcels of land than single people. From 1854 onward, settlers had to pay a small sum for every acre.

- ×**TYPE OF ROUTE** Migration
- ×**MODE OF TRANSPORTATION** Ox cart or mule and horse
- ×**YEAR** Mid-1800s
- ×**DISTANCE** Over 1,800 mi (3,000 km)
- ×**STARTING POINT** Missouri
- ×**END POINT** Oregon City, Oregon
- ×**EST. TIME TO COMPLETE** 5 months

THE NATIVE AMERICANS

The main Native American tribes inhabiting the area around the start of the Oregon Trail were the Cheyenne and the Pawnee. The settlers feared being attacked, but in fact there are numerous accounts of native people helping them lift wagons that had tipped over, rescuing their horses, and bringing them food. The new settlers traded with them, exchanging clothing, tobacco, or weapons for food or horses.

THE TRAIL OF TEARS

For 20 years (1830–50), Native Americans were forced to migrate from their ancestral lands in the southeastern United States to regions west of the Mississippi River. One of the reasons for the relocation was the discovery of gold by the American settlers and the ensuing gold rush that attracted speculators, leading the US government to seize these lands and open them up to settlement. Many native people fell ill and died during the relocation.

LIFE ON THE ROAD

One of the main concerns when setting out on the Oregon Trail was whether there was going to be enough food and drink for the journey. Some of the most commonly consumed foods were rice, beans, bacon, nuts, and pickles. Each wagon carried at least one large barrel of water and some migrants even brought dairy cows with them. The hunting of bison, antelopes, deer, and birds along the way provided another source of food.

DANGERS ALONG THE WAY

The greatest hazard faced by the pioneers was the risk of catching diseases like cholera or dysentery from contaminated food and drinking water. Running out of food or accidents during the journey were other major causes of death.

THE CATHAR TRAIL

The Cathar Trail is located in the south of France. It was the route via which the Cathars were forced into exile during the thirteenth century when the Catholic Church declared their religion heretical. The Cathars, also known as *bons hommes* (good men), suffered persecution right across the region of Occitania (in the south of what today is France). The trail is a historical route filled with impressive castles, many of which are still well preserved.

CARCASSONNE

To visit this city is to travel back in time to the Middle Ages. With its famous Narbonne Gate at the entrance and ramparts including 52 towers, it's one of the best-preserved medieval cities in Europe. Its prominent fortress was declared a Unesco World Heritage site in 1997.

MONTSÉGUR

The Château de Montségur (whose name means "safe mountain") holds great significance in Cathar history as it is the site where the faith's final adherents sought refuge. It's perched atop a kind of rocky hilltop known as a pog, at an elevation of 4,000 feet (1,200 meters) above sea level, and legend has it that the Holy Grail was once housed within its walls.

✕**TYPE OF ROUTE** Migration
✕**MODE OF TRANSPORTATION** On foot
✕**YEAR** Since the 13th century
✕**DISTANCE** Over 125 mi (200 km)
✕**STARTING POINT** Port-la-Nouvelle
✕**END POINT** Foix
✕**EST. TIME TO COMPLETE** 15 days

ALBI

The birthplace of Catharism was Albi. Located on the Tarn River it is also known as the red city due to its blend of stone and brick architecture. Famous landmarks here include the Cathedral of Saint Cecilia, which serves as a monument to the memory of the Cathars, and the impressive Palais de la Berbie.

MINERVE

This small medieval village is perched on the edge of a cliff above the point where the Cesse River meets the Briant. After crossing an impressive viaduct, you enter its narrow streets, where you'll find the Hurepel Museum of Clay Miniatures and the Church of Saint Etienne, all surrounded by a picturesque green landscape.

The Shikoku Pilgrimage is one of the oldest pilgrimage routes in Japan. Its course allows you to visit the 88 temples of the island of Shikoku where the Buddhist monk Kōbō Daishi is thought to have trained or spent time during the ninth century.

This pilgrimage represents the path to enlightenment: temples 1–23 symbolize awakening; temples 24–39 represent austerity and discipline; temples 40–65 represent enlightenment; and temples 66–88 represent reaching nirvana.

THE SHIKOKU PILGRIMAGE
(SHIKOKU HENRO)

- **×TYPE OF ROUTE** Pilgrimage
- **×MODE OF TRANSPORTATION** On foot, by car, or public transport
- **×YEAR** Since the 17th century
- **×DISTANCE** 750 mi (1,200 km)
- **×STARTING POINT** Temple No. 1 Ryōzen-ji
- **×END POINT** Temple No. 88 Ōkubo-ji
- **×EST. TIME TO COMPLETE** 10 days by car, about 2 months on foot, or 12 days by public transport

RYŌZEN-JI TEMPLE (NO. 1)

Located in the city of Naruto, this temple marks the beginning of the pilgrimage. It was founded in the eighth century and its gardens, pagoda, and carp pond are some of its most breathtaking highlights.

CHIKURIN-JI TEMPLE (NO. 31)

Particularly beautiful in spring, this temple is surrounded by greenery. It was built in the eighth century and its five-story pagoda and mountain views are spectacular.

ŌKUBO-JI TEMPLE (NO. 88)

The last of the temples is located in a valley near the border between the prefectures of Kagawa and Tokushima. Inside the temple, you can visit a hall with 88 statues that represent the deities of the temples of the entire pilgrimage.

ONSEN (JAPANESE HOT SPRINGS)

Onsen are thermal baths of volcanic origin. They are an important part of Japanese culture and there are thousands of them throughout the country.

KŪKAI (KŌBŌ DAISHI)

The Buddhist monk, poet, and calligrapher Kūkai (774–835) is known as Kōbō Daishi, meaning Great Master of Buddhist Expansion. He was the founder of Shingon Buddhism (the True Word school) in the ninth century and the creator of the Japanese kana alphabet. He traveled throughout the island of Shikoku in search of spiritual places to meditate. His legend inspired the construction of many temples.

THE MAYA ROUTE

The Maya Route is a circuit that crosses the most important remains of the ancient Mayan civilization, including the ruins of cities and monuments. This route extends through Guatemala, Mexico, and Belize.

QUETZAL

A bird with colorful plumage that inhabits the skies of Central America. Recognizable by its long tail, it was considered a sacred bird by the Maya.

×**TYPE OF ROUTE** Tourist
×**MODE OF TRANSPORTATION** Car, bus, or train
×**DISTANCE** Around 1,300 mi (2,200 km)
×**START AND END** Guatemala
×**EST. TIME TO COMPLETE** Minimum of 15 days; 30 days recommended

CHICHÉN ITZÁ

Located on the Yucatán Peninsula, Mexico, this was one of the most important cities of the Mayan civilization. Among its remains stands the Temple of Kukulcan, an iconic Mayan pyramid that is visited by countless tourists today.

THE MAYA

The Maya were a Mesoamerican civilization that began in about 2,000 BCE and lasted until the early sixteenth century, when they were conquered by the Spanish.

Mayan society was hierarchical and each city was independent from the others. Writing (hieroglyphs), architecture, astronomy, and mathematics were some of the major achievements of Mayan culture, elements of many of which are still in use.

The Maya believed that the universe consisted of three parts: the sky, the Earth, and the underworld.

ROUTE 66

The legendary Route 66, located in the United States, is also known as the Mother Road. It was the highway that connected the Midwest to the West Coast, crossing eight states along the way: Illinois, Missouri, Kansas, Oklahoma, Texas, New Mexico, Arizona, and California. It spanned a total length of 2,448 miles (3,939 kilometers).

In the 1930s, its main purpose was to facilitate the migration of farmers on their way to the West Coast in search of the "promised land." In the 1950s, it became popular among tourists heading for the beach and better weather. With the advent of modern highways, Route 66 was gradually cut out of the official system, but many enthusiasts continue to travel the portions of this road that remain.

- ×**TYPE OF ROUTE** Migration/tourist
- ×**MODE OF TRANSPORTATION** Motor vehicle
- ×**YEAR** Since 1926
- ×**PRESENT** About 85 percent is still accessible
- ×**DISTANCE** 2,448 mi (3,939 km)
- ×**STARTING POINT** Chicago, Illinois
- ×**END POINT** Santa Monica, California
- ×**EST. TIME TO COMPLETE** 2 weeks

THE GRAND CANYON

While there are many scenic views, national parks, and attractions near the route, one of the most awe-inspiring is the Grand Canyon in Arizona. Visited by more than five million people each year, it runs over 277 miles (446 kilometers), reaches depths of up to 5,200 feet (1,600 meters), and exudes a kind of ancestral magic.

The area was once inhabited by Native American tribes such as the Plains, Hualapai, and Navajo, whose settlements were scattered throughout the region. Today, a portion of the canyon is a reservation belonging to the Hualapai people, who fought to have their heritage recognized and their land returned to them.

If you decide to explore the canyon, you can do so by helicopter, white-water raft, or on organized tours.

ON TWO WHEELS

Route 66 is a dream route for motorcyclists. With roaring engines they roll over the asphalt on their adventures.

The actor Marlon Brando's portrayal of Johnny Strabler in the movie *The Wild One* (1953) popularized the typical rebellious biker look.

As you travel along the route, you'll notice the distinctive 1950s aesthetics of the motels, roadside bars, and gas stations.

THE SPICE ROUTES

The Spice Routes, also known as the Maritime Silk Roads, are a network of sea routes that connect the East with the West. They stretch from the west coast of Japan through the islands of Indonesia, around India to the lands of the Middle East, and from there across the Mediterranean to Europe.

- ×**TYPE OF ROUTE** Commercial
- ×**MODE OF TRANSPORTATION** Ship
- ×**YEAR** The first voyage was made by Vasco da Gama in 1498
- ×**DISTANCE** Over 18,000 mi (30,000 km)
- ×**STARTING POINT** Portugal
- ×**END POINT** Japan
- ×**EST. TIME TO COMPLETE** More than 10 months (today around 2 months)

THE MALUKU ISLANDS

Formerly known as the Spice Islands, these form a chain of mountainous islands that stretch across the Pacific Ocean between Sulawesi and New Guinea. They are where cloves and nutmeg originally came from.

FORT COCHIN, KERALA

Merchants from more than 30 countries used the port of Cochin in Kerala (in the south of India). Their ships' hulls were filled with gold that could be traded for the coveted spices, with paprika being the most prized of all. Today, a stroll through the neighborhood of Fort Cochin is a true sensory journey. In the market, the vivid colors of the spices and their enticing aromas attract and captivate visitors.

THE SPICES

These were used to flavor dishes and to help preserve food. They were also used for medicinal purposes due to their antiseptic properties (which means they kill germs). Since it was very challenging to obtain them at the time, they were surrounded by myths and legends.

VASCO DA GAMA (C. 1469–1524)

In 1497, the Portuguese explorer Vasco da Gama set sail with four ships and 170 men in search of a new sea route to India. They circumnavigated Africa and succeeded in reaching Calicut (today's Kozhikode) the following year, going on to make Portugal the leading importer of Eastern spices.

Christopher Columbus was actually also trying to find a new route to India during the same period when he stumbled upon the Americas.

- ×**TYPE OF ROUTE** Commercial/tourist
- ×**MODE OF TRANSPORTATION** Train
- ×**YEAR** The first route opened in 1904
- ×**DISTANCE** Over 5,700 miles (9,000 km)
- ×**STARTING POINT** Moscow (originally)
- ×**END POINT** Vladivostok
- ×**EST. TIME TO COMPLETE** 7 days

PROVODNIZA AND PROVODNIK

Each train car has two attendants who look after the passengers and keep an eye on the train. A female conductor is called a *provodniza* in Russian, and a male conductor is called a *provodnik*.

LAKE BAIKAL

Completely surrounded by mountains, this is the deepest lake in the world and one of the cleanest on the planet.

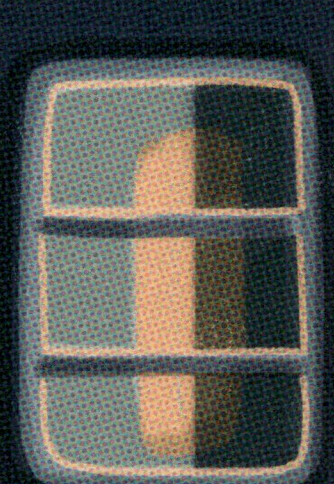

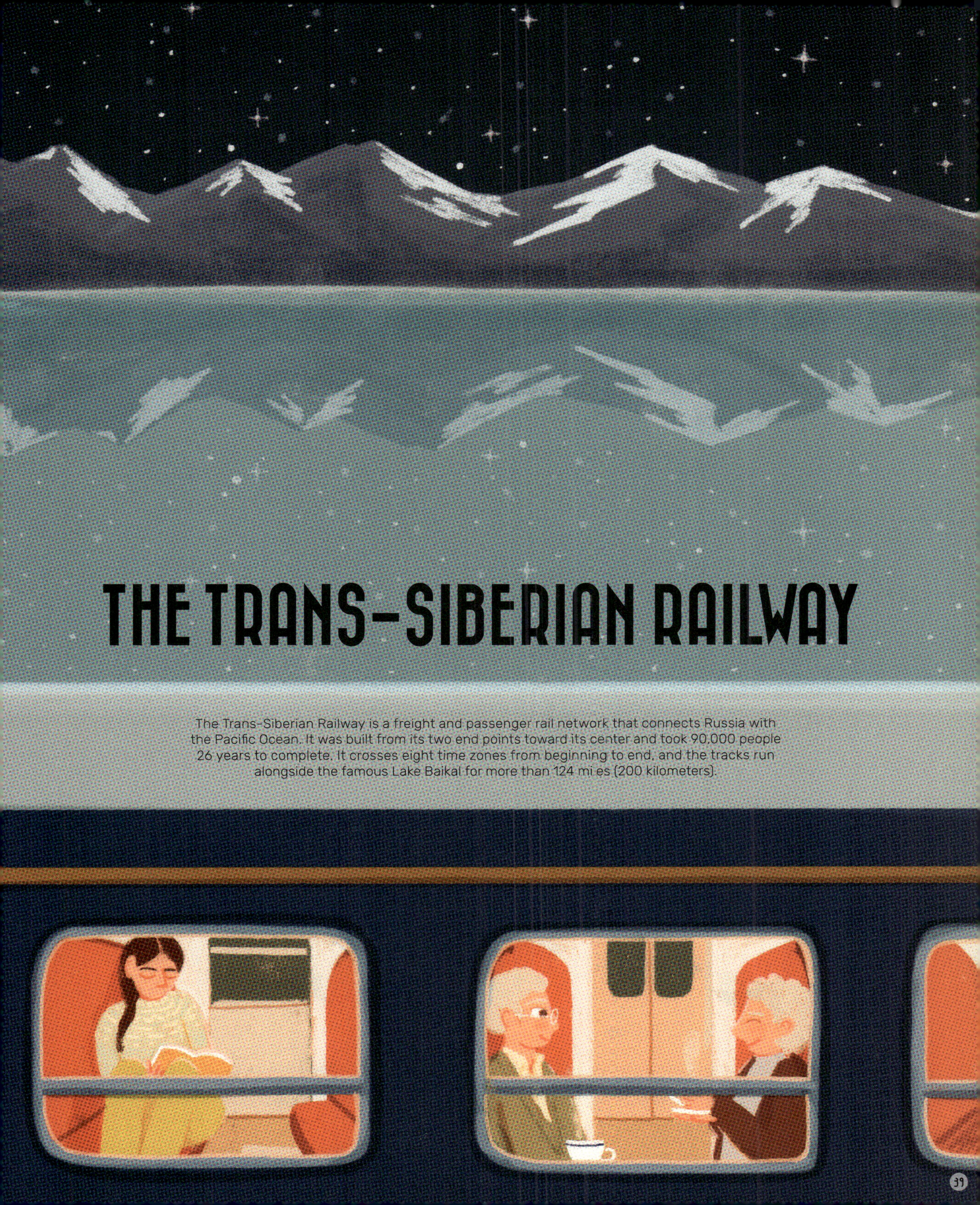

THE TRANS-SIBERIAN RAILWAY

The Trans-Siberian Railway is a freight and passenger rail network that connects Russia with the Pacific Ocean. It was built from its two end points toward its center and took 90,000 people 26 years to complete. It crosses eight time zones from beginning to end, and the tracks run alongside the famous Lake Baikal for more than 124 miles (200 kilometers).

THE INCA TRAIL

× TYPE OF ROUTE Tourist
× MODE OF TRANSPORTATION Public transport or on foot
× DISTANCE 28 mi (45 km)
× STARTING POINT Cusco (also Cuzco)
× END POINT Machu Picchu
× EST. TIME TO COMPLETE 4 days

Today, the Inca Trail is a four-day hike in Peru that connects the Inca capital of Cusco (also spelled Cuzco) with the awe-inspiring citadel of Machu Picchu.

The trail was once part of the Qhapaq Ñan (meaning "main road" in Quechua) and it represented the efforts of the Inca Empire (1200–1533) to unify its territories. It was approximately 19,000 miles (30,000 kilometers) long, stretching across Colombia, Brazil, Ecuador, Peru, and Bolivia, and even reaching the central region of Chile and the northern part of Argentina.

CUSCO

The capital of the Inca Empire, Cusco, in southeastern Peru, is the oldest continuously inhabited city in the Americas and a Unesco World Heritage site. Many of the stone walls found in the city were constructed by the Incas—impressive examples of which can be seen at the fortress of Sacsayhuamán.

PACAYMAYO

Pacaymayo is one of the tributaries of the famous Rio Urubamba, the sacred Incan river that passes through Machu Picchu. Travelers usually stop here on the second day of the trek and it is located at an altitude of about 11,500 feet (3,500 meters).

RUNKURAKAY

On the third day, you would normally encounter this ancient urban and religious site. It would have primarily been used as a lodging *tambo*, or watch post, often by *chasquis* on their journeys, although these way stations were also sites of important ceremonies and rituals.

THE CHASQUIS

The *chasquis* were messengers who were trained from a young age to perform the important postal services of that time. They always carried a *pututu,* a kind of trumpet made from a conch shell, to announce their arrival or request a relay. Using a tangle of knotted strings known as *quipus,* they recorded messages that only they knew how to decipher.

MACHU PICCHU

Perched at an altitude of over 7,900 feet (2,400 meters), this citadel stands as a symbol of Incan culture. Built ir about 1450 BCE, Machu Picchu is a Unesco World Heritage site and one of the most famous sights in the world.

THE NILE RIVER ROUTE

The Nile River has provided fertile land, transportation, food, and fresh water to Egypt for more than 5,000 years. Today, 95 percent of Egypt's population still lives along its banks. Meandering for about 4,130 miles (6,650 kilometers), it is the longest river in the world, followed by the Amazon.

The river played a crucial part in the development of ancient Egypt. In addition to Egypt, the Nile crosses through or borders 10 other African countries. Its three main tributaries are the White Nile, the Blue Nile, and the Atbara.

TRADE IN ANCIENT EGYPT

The river was navigable from Aswan, in the south of the country, to the Mediterranean, and the ancient Egyptians used it for domestic and international trade. For the Egyptians, wood and other construction materials were precious commodities, as they were scarce in the area, so they traded their own grain, pottery, and papyrus in exchange for these.

THEBES

Located on the banks of the Nile, Thebes, or "the city of one hundred gates" (its ruins lie within the modern-day city of Luxor), was the capital of ancient Egypt for more than 1,500 years. The pharaoh Amenophis III ordered his architect Amenhotep to construct the city, which is home to the grand temples of Luxor and Karnak. It served as both a commercial and religious center for the Egyptians, attracting people from all over the world.

THE PHARAOHS

These rulers were believed to be gods in human form and had absolute power over their subjects. Upon their death, they were sometimes buried in chambers inside the pyramids together with their treasures...and their secrets!

× TYPE OF ROUTE Commercial
× MODE OF TRANSPORTATION Ship
× DISTANCE Around 4,000 mi (6,500 km)
× STARTING POINT Lake Victoria, Uganda
× END POINT Mediterranean Sea
× EST. TIME TO COMPLETE 4 months

THE FIRST SAILING BOATS

More than 6,000 years ago, the Egyptians began to sail the waters of the Nile. The boats were constructed using the papyrus plant, the same one used to make paper. Later, the Egyptians used wood. The boats were shaped like a crescent, had a mast, oars, and a square sail, but no keel. Some pharaohs had boats buried with them along with their treasures so that they could sail to the afterlife.

TSITSIKAMMA NATIONAL PARK

This spectacular national park is known for its forests and the water-based activities available here. The different routes you can take to explore its wonders include the Waterfall Trail, the Blue Duiker Trail, and the Mouth Trail.

CANGO CAVES

This network of caves has been around longer than human beings, and it seems that, in the Stone Age, they were inhabited by our ancestors. Rediscovered in 1780 by a local farmer searching for lost animals, they extend over more than 3 miles (5 kilometers) through spacious chambers and narrow corridors, steeped in a silence broken only by our footsteps.

THE GARDEN ROUTE

For those who like to go on a different type of safari, this 186-mile (300-kilometer) route in South Africa passes through mountains and national parks and past beaches and lakes. It is a unique road in this country, along which the beauty of nature can be seen in all its glory. Indeed, the route was added to the Unesco World Heritage List in 2017 as a biosphere reserve.

HERMANUS

The town of Hermanus has an impressive coastline and, during whale season (June to October), southern right whales can be seen migrating through its waters. The sight of these huge, gentle animals greeting each other is unforgettable.

PENGUINS ON THE BEACH?

Boulders Beach, near Cape Town, is home to a colony of African penguins—summer is the best time to observe them. It is estimated that the colony currently numbers between 2,000 and 3,000 penguins.

×TYPE OF ROUTE Tourist
×MODE OF TRANSPORTATION Car
×YEAR Since 2009
×DISTANCE 186 mi (300 km)
×STARTING POINT Mossel Bay
×END POINT Storms River
×EST. TIME TO COMPLETE Between 3 and 14 days